This is my thing

I am a runner. Running is
my thing. It keeps me fit.

I am into books on all sorts of topics. My pal is too.

My sister and I are keen
on chess. You need to
get the king to win.

I am good at art. I am into comics and cartoons.

I am a surfer. It is good to be out in the summer sun.

We are campers. We camp by a river and go fishing too.

I am into cooking. I can cook dinner with my dad.

I am a farmer. Farming is my thing. I feed the hens.

I am a singer. I sing for fun!

I am keen on dogs. It feels
good to be with my dog.

I am a fan of cars. Red
cars, quick cars, all cars.

I am into darts. I aim
for the target.

I was born to be a
rocker. That is my thing.

I am a boxer. I can hit
the bag hard.

Kids are into lots of fun things!

Words to blend

thing	keeps	keen
need	feed	books
good	cook	sorts
born	cartoons	chess
king	singer	fishing
cooking	darts	target
hard	hens	aim

Before reading

Synopsis: There are so many interesting and exciting hobbies we can do to keep healthy and happy. Here are some of the things that might be your thing.

Review graphemes/phonemes: ar or ur ow oi ear air ure

New phoneme: er

Book discussion: Look at the cover and read the title together. Ask: *What are the children on the cover doing?* Talk about the children's own favourite sports and hobbies. Which do they like best, and why?

Link to prior learning: Display the grapheme *er*. Say: *These two letters are a digraph – that means they make one sound.* Write or display these words: *summer, runner, dinner, matter.* How quickly can children spot the *er* digraph and read the words?

Vocabulary check: target – something that you aim at when playing some sports, like darts or archery.

Decoding practice: Display the word *surfer.* Ask children to show you how to split it into two syllables *(s-ur-f/er)* and sound out and blend each syllable in turn to read the word.

Tricky word practice: Display the word *you* and ask children to circle the tricky part of the word (*ou*, which makes a long /oo/ sound). Practise writing and reading this word.

After reading

Apply learning: Ask: *Which two of the hobbies in this book do you like best? Can you think of one similarity between them?*

Comprehension

- Which two hobbies do you think are the most different? Why?

- Which two hobbies do you think are the most similar? Why?

- What do you think the kids on the last page are into?

Fluency

- Pick a page that most of the group read quite easily. Ask them to reread it with pace and expression. Model how to do this if necessary.

- Ask children to choose a favourite page, or double-page spread, and read it with appropriate pace and expression.

- Practise reading the words on page 17.

Tricky words review

my	for	me
into	all	of
and	are	you
the	be	out
was	by	go